Original title:
In the Breeze of the Islands

Copyright © 2025 Creative Arts Management OÜ
All rights reserved.

Author: Derek Caldwell
ISBN HARDBACK: 978-1-80581-529-7
ISBN PAPERBACK: 978-1-80581-056-8
ISBN EBOOK: 978-1-80581-529-7

Lullabies of Gentle Waves

The sea sings softly, a quirky tune,
Crabs dance a jig, under the bright moon.
Seagulls squawk tales of lost potato chips,
As the tide tickles our sandy slips.

A dolphin flips, with a splash and a cheer,
While a fish tells a joke that we barely hear.
The barnacles giggle, they're stuck to the rocks,
As we chase down the waves in our flip-flop socks.

Sand Between Our Toes

With each step we take, the sand hugs tight,
Grains in our shoes, oh what a sight!
A crab scuttles by, in a hurry to flee,
Waving goodbye as if to say, 'Bye, see!'

We build castles tall, with moats just as grand,
Until a wave sneezes and drags them to land.
Laughter erupts, when the buckets all topple,
And a seagull snatches our day's last candy popple.

In the Embrace of Coastal Dreams

The sun wears shades, what a stylish chap,
While we sip from coconuts, take a quick nap.
Turtles in sunglasses, taking the lead,
As we race them down on our goofy green steed.

Waves whisper secrets, like old friends at play,
"Did you hear the one 'bout the fish in the bay?"
We giggle and snort, amidst splashes and grins,
Joining the laughter, where the fun never thins.

Crescendo of the Setting Sun

The sun bows down, painting skies with delight,
As beach balls bounce with all of their might.
A sunset DJ spins tunes on the shore,
Mixing laughter and joy, who could ask for more?

Flip-flops take flight, as the fun starts to swell,
With the sound of a conch, a whimsical bell.
Stars peek out shyly, as night starts to grin,
And we dance on the sand, with the moon as our skin.

Murmurs of the Undercurrents

Seashells gossip on the sand,
They tell tales of a crab so grand.
With tiny glasses and a hat,
He danced around and played with that.

Waves roll in with a splashy cheer,
A fish wearing sunglasses swims near.
It flips and flops in a silly spree,
Said, "Where's the party? Come join me!"

The coconut tree starts to sway,
It shakes off coconuts in a play.
Each nut drops with a playful thud,
A boisterous game in the warm sun's flood.

The parrot squawks with laughter bright,
Pulling pranks in the dim twilight.
With a playful squint and a flair,
It mimics voices, filling the air.

Where Hearts Meet the Shore

Two dolphins leap, a joyful sight,
Playing tag with the fading light.
They share jokes with the flapping seals,
While munching on some tasty meals.

A crab in shorts strolls by with flair,
He struts along without a care.
Sneaky seagulls join in the fun,
Stealing chips, one by one!

The tide rolls back, a playful tease,
As sea oats dance in the balmy breeze.
A sunbather slips with a sassy yell,
The ocean laughs, oh what a swell!

Children giggle, building with sand,
While beach balls bounce, all out of hand.
Laughter mingles with the surf's hum,
Where hearts unite, we all succumb.

Islands Wrapped in Time's Whisper

A turtle donned a tiny tie,
Riding waves as the gulls flew by.
He stopped to trade a fish for ice,
"Delicious!" he said, "Oh, so nice!"

Palms whisper secrets, leaves a-quake,
As iguanas ride a little wake.
Their laughter echoes through the night,
Beneath a sky with stars so bright.

A sandcastle stands, the king's report,
"Beware of waves that may consort!"
But the tide just winks and sweeps away,
Leaving only footprints in the spray.

The island chuckles in the sun,
As we share jokes, oh what fun!
Wrapped in moments, we play and rest,
On this quirky isle, we feel so blessed.

Harmonies in the Canopy

Parrots squawk with zest, they prance,
Bumbling bees join in the dance.
Monkeys chuckle, swinging high,
Who needs a plan? Just let it fly!

Laughter echoes through the leaves,
Tickled by the playful thieves.
Squirrels share their nutty jokes,
While palm fronds sway with sunny pokes!

Laughter Carried by Ocean Zephyrs

Waves crash with a splashy cheer,
As crabs scuttle, quick to sneer.
Sea turtles take a slow, soft dive,
While fish wear fins, seeming to jive.

Seagulls squawk a silly tune,
Dancing 'round with a bright cartoon.
Flip-flops flop as folks stroll by,
Under the watchful, grinning sky.

Driftwood Tales and Tropical Nights

Driftwood castles line the shore,
Where seashells tell tales and more.
Fireflies twinkle, join the chat,
While hermit crabs wear hats, imagine that!

A starfish tells a knock-knock joke,
As laughter bubbles, chords evoke.
With coconut drinks, and smiles so bright,
This night feels like pure delight!

Shadows of Coconut Trees

Coconuts drop with a thud so loud,
Making beachgoers laugh, quite proud.
A crab in shades struts on the sand,
With a swagger only the sun can withstand!

Under the shade, stories unfold,
Of mermaids knitting and pirates bold.
As shadows stretch and day turns to night,
The world's a circus, what a sight!

Breeze-Swept Secrets of Coastal Gardens

A squirrel wearing shades, so cool,
Dances on the fence, thinks it's a pool.
The flowers giggle as they sway,
Whispering secrets in a cheeky way.

A flamingo tries to mimic a duck,
Stepping on toes, oh what luck!
The garden gnomes are holding a parade,
Laughing at the lobster in its charade.

The Language of Winds Between Islands.

The wind tells tales to the seashells bright,
Of crabs that tango in the moonlight.
With every gust, a story unfolds,
Of fish that wear boots, oh so bold.

Seagulls chatter like gossiping friends,
While the waves nod, making amends.
They sneak in jokes from the ocean's deep,
While islanders laugh, barely awake from sleep.

Whispers of the Palm Trees

The palms gossip with the sun above,
Sharing tales of a turtle in love.
They sway and roll like laughter's delight,
While the coconuts cheer with sheer delight.

A chameleon dons a grass skirt so fine,
Twisting and twirling, feeling divine.
For every rustle, a joke takes flight,
As the day fades gently into night.

Tides of Gentle Memories

The tide rolls in with a quirky wave,
Bringing back moments that we all crave.
A crab's tap dance goes out of sync,
While the seaweed giggles, oh what a wink!

Old flip-flops recount their wild days,
In the salty air, they reminisce plays.
With each wave crashing, a laugh they share,
In the soft sandy sunshine, with nary a care.

Tranquil Ebb in Hidden Coves

Waves whisper secrets to the sand,
A crab attempts a waltz, so grand.
Seagulls squawk and dive for a chip,
While dolphins giggle on their trip.

Palm trees sway, they dance and swing,
Coconuts drop with a thud and zing.
The sun sneezes, the ocean laughs,
As fish swim by in their funny gaffs.

Choreography of Wind and Wave

The wind's got moves, a lively spin,
It tousles the hair of a grinning kin.
Shells do the tango upon the shore,
While flip-flops struggle to keep the score.

The waves break out in a hearty cheer,
Splashing the folks who wander near.
A crab moonwalks, with style so bold,
As sunbathers shrug, tired of the heat's hold.

Island Rhythms Beneath the Stars

Stars waltz in the sky, all aglow,
The moon's a spotlight for the dreamiest show.
Fireflies wink like they're in on a joke,
While the night air whispers, 'Let's have a poke!'

A turtle tries to breakdance, oh dear,
Its moves, let's say, could use some more cheer.
The owls hoot, but they sound like a band,
Joining the laughter of the sea and land.

Ferns and Fables by the Shore

Ferns tickle toes on a sandy patch,
As kids build castles, planning their hatch.
A crab in a crown takes his royal stance,
While a parrot squawks, calling for a dance.

Old tales are spun in whispers so light,
Of mermaids who giggle at the moon's bright.
Fish tell stories of their daring escape,
While sea urchins giggle, but can't form a shape.

Palms Swaying to Nature's Symphony

The palms wave gently, oh what a sight,
They dance like chickens in midday light.
With hats askew and coconuts near,
Even the crabs join in without fear.

A rhythm of rustles, a giggling crowd,
As seagulls squawk, feeling too proud.
The beach ball bounces, a fun little game,
While sandcastles flop with no one to blame.

Flip-flops flying, a chase for a drink,
Oh, how the sun makes us all stop and think.
With laughter and splashes, we create a cheer,
As the sun dips low, bringing night ever near.

Stories Carved by the Trade Winds

Whispers of tales float on the air,
A sunburned pirate with mismatched footwear.
He says he once found a treasure so bright,
But it turned out to be just a kids' kite.

The winds tell secrets, a tickling jest,
While fish on the line take a big rest.
Shells do the cha-cha upon the warm sand,
As a crab convinces the waves he's a band.

With long-nosed seagulls talking their shmack,
They argue about who can make the best snack.
Life in the surf brings stories anew,
And every evening, we tell them to you.

A Canvas of Colors in Ocean's Light

The sunset splatters shades of bright hue,
Like a painter who drank too much brew.
Pink and orange in a wild embrace,
Even the dolphins join in the race.

Crabs in bow ties dance to a tune,
A surfboard oddity chased by the moon.
Frogs with surfboards make quite the scene,
They flip and they flop like they've never been.

As colors blend and laughter ignites,
The seaweed wiggles, enjoying the nights.
With jokes from the waves, our spirits take flight,
An evening of color — oh, what a delight.

Celestial Dances on Rippling Waters

Stars twinkle, laughing at waves below,
As mermaids giggle with a shimmering glow.
They splash around, showing off their flair,
With starfish applauding — oh, what a pair!

The moon takes center stage, a bright disco ball,
Making shadows dance, calling all to the call.
A crab in a tutu steals the whole show,
While fishes all murmur, "Can you believe this glow?"

The night drips magic, fun overflows,
Sea turtles do cartwheels, the audience grows.
The ocean's our stage, and we laugh till we cry,
In a waltz with the cosmos, feeling free as we fly.

Of Gypsy Winds and Starry Skies

Blowing hats from heads majestic,
Chasing crabs, oh so fantastic.
The moon wears a grin so wide,
While dolphins laugh, and waves collide.

Genies tease reluctant boats,
Sandcastles built with funny moats.
Seagulls squawk their funny tunes,
As a fish dons a pair of loons.

With every gust, a new delight,
Kite strings dance in the soft moonlight.
A coconut drops, it's quite absurd,
Nutty antics make the locals stir.

Breezy tales are shared at dusk,
Laughter echoes, a joyful husk.
Under the stars, friendships grow,
In the lighthearted ebb and flow.

Shoreline Stories of Yesterday

Old flip-flops chase the tide,
As tales of the past slide and glide.
The fish once told of great escapes,
But lost their pride to a net of shapes.

Sandy toes, what a fancy feel,
As seagulls steal your lunchtime meal.
A story of shells tucked in a sack,
Each one whispers tales, no lack.

A chicken joins the picnic feast,
Stealing crumbs, it's quite the beast.
Stories linger on salty lips,
Phone cameras caught all the quips.

Time ticks by in a sunny blur,
Where past and present twist and stir.
Laughter ripples through the air,
In quirky moments we all share.

Heartbeats in the Mist of Morning

Morning coffee's airborne flight,
As seagulls plot their daring bites.
The mist hugs tightly like a friend,
Meanwhile, postman's bike won't bend.

A surfboard plays with a sleepy dog,
While locals jog past without a fog.
Misty cries from shellfish grumpy,
As tourists smile feeling quite bumpy.

What's that lurking in the bay?
A lobster ready for a dance today.
Beach towels fight for sunny ground,
Lost flip-flops squeak with every sound.

Coconuts tumble with a thud,
Ending laughter in the morning mud.
Breezy stories wake the land,
With funny quirks by nature planned.

Tethered to the Gentle Current

Rafts float by in a silly race,
Chasing smiles, splashes, and grace.
The breeze comes in with mischief fair,
It tousles hair and ruffles air.

Bubbles pop like laughter bright,
As snorkelers dive, well out of sight.
A crab in a tutu scuttles fast,
Waving goodbye to his sandy past.

Paddles splash, a symphony's tune,
As time reveals the dance of June.
Flip-flops find their proper place,
In stables of shells, a funny space.

Waves tell tales of wacky ventures,
Where no one knows the right indentures.
Life's a game in this floating fun,
Tethered hearts under the warm sun.

The Sigh of an Ocean Breeze

A seagull landed with a thud,
He thought he'd win a crab feast, good!
But crabs just waved, all claws on guard,
His plans of lunch were deeply marred.

The waves chuckled, rolling in,
'Your fishing skills? Oh, where to begin!'
With a ruffled feather, he raised his beak,
'At least I'm better than that old antique!'

Alongside the Driftwood's Tale

A piece of wood called out for friends,
'Let's have a party, where the fun never ends!'
But all the driftwood just laughed and lay,
'We've been here too long, please don't make us stay!'

With a bob and a weave, the tide had its say,
'Join me for a splash, it's a beach holiday!'
But driftwood remained with sunburned skin,
Dreaming of adventures that never begin.

Reflections of Celestial Stars

Stars twinkled down with a wink and a grin,
'Who's ready for fun? Let the night race begin!'
The moon just laughed, spinning in glee,
'Just try not to fall into the sea!'

A comet zipped past with a bright, flashy pull,
'I'm here for a laugh, and my orbit's quite full!'
But the stars just sparkled and grooved with delight,
As meteors crashed, with a bang! What a sight!

Whispers of Forgotten Tides

The old tide pool bragged to the shore,
'Once I held treasures, oh, so much more!'
But shells just giggled, rolling like marbles,
'Now you're just home to those wiggly garbles!'

'My waters were deep, my tales ever grand!'
The barnacles grinned, 'We'll lend you a hand!'
With shouts of laughter, they splashed all around,
As wisdom dissolved with every wave sound.

Sheltered Within Nature's Arms

Under palm trees, a squirrel dances,
Chasing coconuts, taking chances.
A parrot squawks a silly tune,
While crabs march like they own the moon.

The waves giggle, teasing the shore,
Inviting splashes, begging for more.
A sunburned tourist tries to impress,
Trips on his towel, oh what a mess!

Fish swim by with a wink and nod,
As we build castles, the sand feels odd.
A sandcastle smirks at a passing fluke,
Well, the tide's got this, let's not rebuke!

With laughter echoing under the sun,
The joy of folly is second to none.
So here's to the moments, hilarious, bright,
In nature's embrace, everything's right!

Revelations at the Island's Edge

A seagull steals my sandwich away,
I chase it, shouting, 'That's not okay!'
The beach chairs tango, swaying with glee,
As if the ocean hosts a wild jubilee.

The horizon stretches like a lazy cat,
A beach ball rolls off with a soft spat.
Children giggle, gathering shells, oh my,
Don't tell them, but some look like pies!

Sunburned tourists complain and pout,
But the sunbeam's dance never leaves doubt.
Flip-flops fly when the waves come near,
Splashing laughter, mingled with cheer.

Out of the blue, a crab starts to waltz,
As we join in—we're happy, no faults.
With the beach as our stage, we embrace the fun,
Laughing together, our spirits outrun!

The Solace of the Indigo Wave

A dolphin pokes its head with charm,
While I'm settling in, safe from harm.
Sand takes a vacation on my big toe,
And the mermaids giggle, putting on a show.

Seashells whisper secrets from deep,
The kind that make you laugh, or lose sleep.
As seagulls squawk in their own little bands,
I try to catch jokes, but they slip through my hands.

The sun's a prankster, feels too bright,
While drinks wobble like a drunken kite.
Crabs gather round for a dinner plate,
Surprising the gull, who's now late for fate.

With waves rolling in and laughter out,
Every moment here is a new route.
In the playful sea, with each chant and wave,
We cherish the joy that the tide will save.

Nurtured by the Sea's Fraction

A tiny fish zooms by with a smile,
While I'm building my fort, getting cozy in style.
With every splash, my heart feels light,
Even the seaweed dances tonight!

A hermit crab moves in its new shell,
Thinking it's grand—can't you tell?
The sun sets, painting stories so bright,
As I chuckle, my worries take flight.

Friends try to surf—oh what a sight!
Balance is key but they're losing the fight.
Like rubber ducks tossed in a tide,
With waves of laughter, we take our pride.

The salty air fills my lungs with glee,
In this funny slice of the open sea.
So here we flourish, in joy we connect,
In nature's carnival, we find perfect!

Songs of the Windswept Shores

Seagulls squawk on a sunny day,
Dodging tourists who laugh and sway.
Sandcastles built with a bucket and grin,
Watch out for the wave, here comes the win!

Flip-flops flung in a playful dance,
Toes in the surf, they take their chance.
Ice cream drips down an eager chin,
Life's a game where we all can win!

Sun hats blown by the cheeky gust,
Finding treasures in sun-warmed rust.
Each whisper of ocean tells a tale,
Of mermaids dancing beneath the veil!

Kites flying high with colors so bright,
Chasing each other in a playful flight.
Laughter echoes, it's what we choose,
To run with the wind, we simply can't lose!

Echoes of Laughter and Light

Bubbles float in the golden sun,
Children giggle, oh what fun!
Sand crabs scuttle in a frantic race,
Who will win, the sand or the chase?

Picnics scattered on plaid and mat,
Ants parade, each wearing a hat!
Jokes crackle like the waves nearby,
As sun-kissed clouds dance in the sky.

Watermelon smiles with seeds to spit,
Try not to laugh, oh just don't quit!
A sand pail hats off to clever dreams,
Whispers float on the mischievous beams.

The sun sets low, a painter's brush,
Evening brings on a gentle hush.
With jest and cheer, our hearts ignite,
In laughter's glow, everything feels right!

Radiance at Dusk's Embrace

Twilight's charm, it hugs so tight,
Fireflies dance in the fading light.
Laughter spills like a running stream,
As friends gather to share a dream.

Stars peek out, adorned in glee,
Who's got the best joke? Let's see!
Marshmallows toast over crackling fire,
While shadows grow in our hearts' desire.

With each s'more, delight's unfold,
Sticky fingers, stories told.
The ocean's whisper, a playful tease,
As everyone fights to get the last cheese!

Giggles float in the cooling air,
Under the night sky, a joy to share.
Smiles light up as stars ignite,
Embraced by the dusk, it feels so right!

Drifting Dreams on Salt-Kissed Air

Surfboards wobble with a silly splash,
Riding the waves with a giggling crash.
Cool lemonade mixed with laughter sweet,
Life is a dance, on the sandy street.

Tents pop up like mushrooms at dawn,
Breezes rustle, and shadows yawn.
Flip-flops fly in a game of catch,
Friendly competition, let's see who'll hatch!

Sandy faces, brightened hearts,
A child's laughter, where the fun starts.
As night descends, lanterns gleam,
Our memories woven, it feels like a dream.

So let the waves serenade our cheer,
With tales of joy, forever dear.
Under the stars, with spirits so rare,
Drifting together in the salt-kissed air!

Oceanside Reflections of the Soul

Waves crash, and seagulls squawk,
The beach ball rolls, an awkward walk.
Sunburned noses, funny sights,
Chasing ice cream, pure delights.

Bikini mishaps, a flip-flop flies,
Sand stuck where it shouldn't lie.
Kids giggle at the dad's wild dance,
As the tide comes in, a comical chance.

Beach umbrellas bend and sway,
Dancing shadows through the day.
The sound of laughter, waves that tease,
Life is a show, with laughter's ease.

Flights of Fancy on the Gossamer Wind

Kites soar high, colors clash,
With a tip of the hat, they make a splash.
Windy whispers beneath the sun,
While tacos fly, what a fun run!

Squirrels plotting, a cheeky crew,
Stealing snacks, in this zoo.
A rogue flip-flop sails away,
As giggles burst like a sprightly spray.

A breeze carries voices, cheers and sighs,
Each flight an adventure, beneath the skies.
With laughter wrapped in sunshine bold,
Memories made, more precious than gold.

The Twilight Between Day and Night

A sunset spills its orange flair,
As crickets tune their night affair.
Flip-flops squeak on wooden decks,
As old jokes fly like silly wrecks.

Fireflies waltz in a dance so bright,
While grandpa snorts and tells of fright.
Marshmallows melt on sticks of wood,
Each toast a giggle, all's for good.

Stars blink down, a twinkle's tease,
As shadows stretch with playful ease.
In this twilight, fun reigns supreme,
A world of dreams, both odd and gleam.

Dreams Written in the Sand

Footprints lead with silly grace,
As waves erase their playful trace.
A castle leans, just can't stand still,
Shells giggle, sharing their thrill.

Messages scribbled all askew,
A heart, a smile, the ocean's view.
The tide teases with a sly retreat,
In the sand, fun stories meet.

Laughter echoes, joy on this strand,
A treasure hunt for dreams at hand.
With every wave, a new chance brings,
Silly sketches of all our things.

The Language of Falling Leaves

Leaves chatter softly, full of glee,
Playing tag with the dancing sea.
A squirrel debates with a cheeky crow,
As acorns fall like nature's throw.

Whispers of rustling, a playful tease,
Each leaf spirals down with elegant ease.
A rhythm of laughter, the trees take flight,
While bugs wear tiny hats, oh what a sight!

Pumpkin spice aromas float on the wind,
Even the grass seems to grin and spin.
Footsteps crunching like a snack divine,
Nature's confetti, oh what a time!

So gather 'round, let the laughter swell,
Each falling leaf seems to cast a spell.
In this symphony of rustles and curls,
Who knew that nature had such twirls?

Twilight's Soft Embrace on Water

As day hugs night, they dance and sway,
The fish are laughing in their own play.
A moonbeam trip, like a playful jester,
Makes the waves giggle, oh what a tester!

Crabs wear tiny glasses, sipping their tea,
Conspiracies whispered by the old banyan tree.
In this watery world where silliness flows,
Even the seaweed puts on a show!

Stars join the party with a twinkle and wink,
While mermaids practice their grand clink.
Shells sing ballads of beaches and tides,
Holding secrets where laughter abides.

With twilight's brush, the story unfolds,
Tickling the waters, and stories retold.
So let's toast the dusk, in splashes and glee,
In this nightly carnival of jubilee!

Serenity Wrapped in Warm Whispers

Pineapple hats line the ocean's shore,
As flip-flops plop—who could ask for more?
A hammock sways with a giggle and squeak,
Birds serenade, with tunes ever cheek.

Coconuts gossip while sipping their drinks,
Even the sandcastles smile as they blink.
Sunsets laugh in shades of peach and gold,
Echoing secrets that the waves have told.

Shells chatter, nesting all snug and tight,
Crickets play symphonies throughout the night.
The stars come out wearing their best,
Swaying in rhythm, reveling in rest.

Each breath is a snicker, sweet and clear,
Happiness whispers, inviting us near.
Wrapped in this joy, let tranquil thoughts flow,
Chasing the giggles wherever we go!

Journeying Through Turquoise Dreams

A sailboat hums with a cartoonish grin,
Each wave a chuckle, as we begin.
Dolphins pop up, wearing cool shades,
Turning the sea into circus parades!

The sun wears a crown of wobbly rays,
Tickling the ocean in playful displays.
Seashells relaying tales of old,
With snorts of laughter, and secrets bold.

We float like clouds in a whimsical tale,
Where fish wear bow ties, and no one is frail.
On this turquoise canvas, our dreams take flight,
In a laughter-filled journey, day turns to night.

So grab your compass, let silliness soar,
With each gentle breeze, we crave for more.
A celebration of fun, where joy beams,
Adrift in these vibrant, turquoise dreams!

The Caress of Distant Shores

Palm trees dance with a giggle,
Seagulls swoop, their wings in a wiggle.
Laughter echoes through the air,
Flip-flops flying everywhere.

Tides tickle toes at the edge,
Sandcastles lean, a funny hedge.
Sunburns create the silliest sights,
Even the crabs prance in their fights.

With coconuts crackling like jokes,
Beach balls bouncing off playful folks.
Hammocks swing with a lazy cheer,
And fish whisper tales to your ear.

So grab a drink, let joy abound,
Every wave brings laughter around.
In riotous fun, we shall dwell,
As nature's comedy casts its spell.

Currents of Memory and Sand

Waves tell secrets in a playful tone,
Sand flies up from a lost sandal's throne.
Moons in the shell hold stories so bright,
While children chase crabs in their kite-fueled flight.

A jellyfish dances in jiggly delight,
And sunhats are lost, oh what a sight!
Seashells giggle, they're shy, you see,
Whispers of oceanic filigree.

Fishermen dream of a catch so grand,
Only for seagulls to steal from their hand.
The sunbeams joke, "Don't be a slouch,"
While waves giggle, "Come take a crouch!"

Memory drifts like driftwood afloat,
Knowing laughter will always promote.
With every grain of sand in your shoe,
You'll find the funny in all that's true.

Sunsets Wrapped in Ocean's Embrace

The horizon blushes, a carpet of fun,
With colors that race like they're on the run.
Dolphins leap with a wink and a grin,
Their splashes echo a bubbly din.

Palm leaves sway to a bouncy beat,
While sunset colors make daydreams sweet.
Faint giggles slip on the evening tide,
As starfish conspire on the shoreline's side.

Beach bonfires crackle with stories of yore,
Marshmallows toast—who could ask for more?
The sky is a canvas, each hue a prank,
As the moon dips low with a luminous prank.

Joy drifts on waves, in a swirl of light,
Chasing the laughs that dance out of sight.
Let's caper through dusk, on this shore so bright,
In the ocean's embrace, everything feels right.

Veils of Mist on Coral Coastlines

Morning mist teases the eye with a sigh,
As fishy puns swim swiftly by.
Coral reefs giggle with colors so bold,
Playing hide and seek in their underwater fold.

Winds whisper tales that tickle your ear,
Of mermaids lost in their jovial cheer.
Sand dollars shell out hilarious dreams,
While crabs do their dance in impossible seams.

Seashells, like laughter, are treasures untold,
Each one a secret, a memory to hold.
With the tide rolling in for a giggly play,
Even in mist, fun's the best way to stay.

As sunsets emerge from their thicket of grey,
Every moment reminds us to laugh and to sway.
So take a deep breath, let joy take its course,
For on this coastline, we find our own source.

Sunsets Over Silent Waters

Golden glow on water's face,
Seagulls dance, a silly race.
Crabs in costumes, bold and bright,
Join the party, what a sight!

Flip-flops flying, toes in play,
Sunset laughter, come what may.
A jellyfish with goofy glee,
Waves whisper secrets, wild and free.

Drinks in hand, the parrots squawk,
A banana boat starts to rock.
Sandy socks and silly hats,
Ocean foam and playful chats.

As the day bids soft retreat,
Clams laugh loud; they can't be beat.
A hermit crab tries on a shoe,
Sunsets here are never blue!

Celestial Shores and Oceanic Secrets

Under stars, the beach is bright,
Dancing crabs, oh what a sight!
Octopuses twirl, arms in air,
A conch shell whispers, 'Don't you dare!'

Turtles waddle with a hop,
Chasing moonbeams, can't you stop?
Seashells giggle, spread the news,
The ocean's full of funny clues.

Pirates search for treasure near,
But end up trading glee for beer.
Mermaids giggle, what a show,
Waving fins in gentle flow.

Sandcastles made with care and cheer,
Join the sand fight, never fear!
A coconut laughs, it rolls away,
On shores where dreams and jokes play.

Footprints in the Grain of Time

Footprints leading, all askew,
Little ones chase, splashing too.
The tide's receding, belly flops,
While dad's stuck with soggy socks.

Seashells here have tales to share,
Hidden giggles in the air.
Little fish play hide and seek,
While beach balls roll and seagulls squeak.

The old dock creaks a funny tune,
As kids spin 'round beneath the moon.
Sand in sandwiches, what a mess!
But laughter's gold; it's pure finesse.

With every grain a story's spun,
Playing tag till day is done.
In footprints left by carefree times,
The ocean sings in giggling chimes.

Currents of Solitude and Surrender

Alone, but laughing with the tide,
Whales do flips; oh what a ride!
Seashells hum a quirky tune,
While starfish dance under the moon.

Here's a beach where solitude reigns,
But every wave brings funny gains.
The breeze plays tricks, a playful tease,
Seagulls steal fries with crafty ease.

Pineapple hats and shifty eyes,
Every splash comes with a surprise.
Waves hug the shore, a sweet embrace,
Fishes giggle, showing their face.

So with laughter in the heart,
I find joy in this funny part.
Currents pull, but I won't yield,
With humor, my spirit is healed.

Harmony of Wind and Water

Waves tickle toes, giggles soar,
A seagull steals fries, but we want more.
Sandcastles lean, a royal mess,
The tide comes in, oh what distress!

Cool drinks spill, we laugh and shout,
A crab sidesteps, takes the route.
Jumping high, we chase the shade,
While beach balls roll, our plans cascade.

Kooky hats fly, off into the air,
Sand in our shoes, without a care.
Friends gather 'round, the stories grow,
From silly dances, to rolling slow.

With each breeze, a joke unfolds,
Life's little treasures, worth more than gold.
The rhythm of fun, we can't ignore,
As laughter waves back from the shore.

Lighthouses of Lost Stories

Old lighthouses wink, like an eye,
Beacons of tales beneath the sky.
Ghost ships drift and charms they share,
While gulls make faces, full of flair.

Fish swim by in glasses of gin,
A shipwreck dance, where to begin?
The captain's hat is far too large,
Mysterious warning, no need to charge.

Tales of mermaids, amusing and bold,
With fish that tease, so never grow old.
The sailor's laugh, a comical tune,
Echoes at dusk, beneath the moon.

Waves whistle secrets, breezes hum,
Sandwiches vanish, a strange conundrum.
Lost in the tales, our hearts will play,
As laughter lights up yet another day.

Serenades of the Soulful Nautilus

Bubbles dance in a madcap spree,
Nautilus sings, mysteriously.
Tentacles wave, a curious sight,
In this underwater, bizarre delight.

Jellyfish jiggle as they float swift,
While fish tell tales, a playful gift.
The seaweed sways, a disco ball,
A creature's dance, we dare not stall.

With shells as hats, we join the show,
Crabs tap dance, putting on a glow.
Oceans chuckle with every splash,
Where laughter mixes in a joyful crash.

As tides tease lightly, bright and free,
The soul of the sea invites the spree.
Underwater ballads, we can't resist,
In this quirky rhythm, life's a twist!

A Dance of Sea and Sky

Clouds tumble down, laughing so loud,
While sunlight glimmers, beneath a cloud.
Kites soar high, dashing like dreams,
Painting the air with whimsical beams.

Ocean waves clap, a rhythmic cheer,
As beach umbrellas spin without fear.
Merry umbrellas, what a sight,
As they chase the wind in pure delight.

Gulls hold court, in a feathered spree,
With each looping dive, they shout with glee.
Twisted tales told by the tide,
A comic ballet where jokes abide.

From dawn to dusk, the dance won't cease,
Creating joy, a timeless piece.
With every gust that sweeps on by,
Life's perfect punchline, beneath the sky.

Sunlit Isles and Gentle Currents

On shores where crabs have dance contests,
And seagulls steal your lunchtime quests.
Palm trees sway like they're on a spree,
Chasing each other, wild and free.

The waves wear hats of frothy white,
Tickling toes, what a delight!
Shells gossip secrets, all quite absurd,
While fish swim by, laughing unheard.

With sunblock on, I slip and slide,
Chasing my drink, it's quite the ride!
Tiki torches sway with a cheesy grin,
As I trip over my own sandal pin.

So here we laugh under the sun's ray,
Making memories that won't fade away!
With every giggle, the day feels right,
In this paradise, our hearts take flight.

Serenade of the Seafoam

The seafoam sings a bubbly song,
While flip-flops squeak along the throng.
Crabs do the cha-cha, oh what a sight,
As I try to dance, but get it all quite tight.

The sun can roast, but so can my fries,
I wave to the chef; he just replies.
An octopus joins for a game of chess,
With tentacles waving, he's quite the mess.

Coconut drinks with tiny umbrellas,
Made me think of all the Gordon Gellas.
As I sip, a parrot squawks with glee,
"The best drink's found under this palm tree!"

So here we sway with laughter and cheer,
In this lively place where fun is sincere.
With each wave's laughter, life we adore,
Singing sweet songs of joy on the shore.

Wings of the Trade Winds

The trade winds giggle, playfully loud,
As beach umbrellas dance in a crowd.
A toucan jokes, "I'm the funniest bird!"
While I just trip, my antics absurd.

A hammock swings, but I just flop,
Mistaken for a seal on a big old mop.
The sun waves hello, with a wink so sly,
As a dolphin jumps, catching the sky.

The beach ball bounces, but I can't keep,
Chasing it down, I'm in way over my leap.
Laughter rings out from every nook,
As I land in the sand with just one look.

With each gust, our spirits soar,
As laughter and joy burst through the shore.
So raise a toast to the fun we find,
In this wild world, let's leave worries behind.

Island Dreams on Coral Shores

In a land where dreams and laughter collide,
Turtle races happen by the tide.
Lobsters wear caps, strutting on the sand,
Thinking they're kings, it's all quite grand.

Mermaids giggle, brushing their hair,
While I dive in, splashing everywhere.
A crab comments, "What a sight to see!"
As I come up, sunburned but carefree.

Under the palms, the stories unfold,
Of pirate treasure and tacos sold.
With every chuckle, the day feels bright,
As the moon waves hello, preparing for night.

So let's embrace this island spree,
Where fun and laughter flow like the sea.
With each memory made, we'll savor the glee,
In this wondrous realm, just you and me.

Veiled Secrets of the Isle's Heart

A coconut fell with a splat,
A squirrel jumped, oh what a chat!
The tour guide danced, a sight so rare,
While locals laughed without a care.

Seagulls squawked a cheeky song,
As beach balls bounced, all day long.
Sunburned tourists all around,
In flip-flops twirling on the ground.

A crab wore shades and strutted by,
While sunbathers let out a sigh.
With every wave, a giggle's push,
As surfboards tried to catch a crush.

Yet secret tales beneath the sun,
Of mermaids' laughter, pure fun begun.
In every twist, each splash, each howl,
The isle reveals its joy, so foul!

Memory's Echo on the Tidal Edge

Footprints fading, what a curious sight,
As crabs disguised as kings steal the light.
Beachcomber's hat blew off with a twirl,
Chasing it down made the seagulls whirl.

A wave crashed loud, a splashy dance,
Ice creams toppled, oh, not by chance!
Children giggled as sand flew high,
While dolphins jumped with a cheeky sigh.

Shells whispered secrets in salty air,
Of pirate treasures buried with care.
But all they found were jellyfish stings,
And a lost shoe that once danced with kings.

In this raucous place, oh what a fun,
The memories made can't be outrun.
With every echo, giggles resound,
As the tide sings stories, so profound.

Harmony Born From Salt and Sand

A ukulele strummed with a clumsy flair,
While beachgoers danced without a care.
Sandy toes and laughter silly,
As fish tried to swim through a jelly!

The tide rolled in with a splashy cheer,
As kids made castles, drawing near.
But who knew buckets could get so mad,
When waves decided to join the fad?

Neighbors bickered over a chair,
While crabs made plans in their secret lair.
But all disagreements washed away,
With waves that giggled, come what may.

So laughter echoed through palms so tall,
As sun-kissed enjoying their endless ball.
In the rhythm of salt and sandy lands,
Joyful harmonies live, oh so grand!

Petals in the Wind

Petals floated on a warm, soft gust,
As sunhats twirled in a playful rust.
Kids chased scents of ocean spray,
While chickens strutted, hip-hip-hooray!

A parrot squawked with cheeky flair,
Stealing snacks from a tourist's pair.
The wind whistled through the palm fronds,
As laughter bubbled like fresh-made ponds.

Drifting leaves, a colorful flight,
As party hats began the night.
With every twist of the joyful dance,
Nature giggled, giving chance.

So join the chorus of echoing cheer,
With petals swirling, please come near!
Let sunshine guide our wayward souls,
For fun blooms wild as each heart rolls!

Essence of Island Spirit

Palm trees sway with a grin,
While coconuts try to spin.
Seagulls squawk with a silly cheer,
As fish tell tales that we can hear.

Flip-flops slapping on sandy ground,
Crabs in a race, trying to be crowned.
A sunburned tourist, bright as a fire,
Complains about the island's attire.

Tiki torches flicker, shadows dance,
While pineapples watch a romance.
Loud laughter floats, it's hard to miss,
As island vibe sends you to bliss.

With each wave, a chuckle flows,
Jellyfish wear hats, but no one knows.
Here life's a joke, let worries cease,
In a land where giggles never decrease.

Farewell To Distant Shores

Goodbye to the sun, we'd dance and play,
With sand in our shoes, we'd sway all day.
A crab waved 'bye, but tripped on a shell,
Seashells laughing, casting their spell.

The sky paints pink, a farewell light,
As seagulls boast about their flight.
Flip-flops forgotten, lost in the tide,
While beach chairs fold up, where dreams reside.

Mangoes roll down, escaping their fate,
Chasing the waves on a plate so great.
We wave our arms, a comic lament,
As our island fun's in a different rent.

Farewell to the fiends of the sun-kissed shore,
But laughter remains, we'll come back for more.
Witty memories tucked in our bags,
Leaving behind our sun-sparkled rags.

Emblems of the Horizon's Hope

A horizon wide, where dreams collide,
With jellybeans sailing, what a ride!
Dolphins delight in a playful chase,
As tiki gods keep a smiling face.

Hopes like kites, soaring up high,
While the breezes join in a joyful sigh.
A coconut sings a tune so sweet,
As waves clap hands, keeping the beat.

Mirthful clouds gather, plotting their fun,
Splashing color like confetti from the sun.
Every horizon, a chuckle of cheer,
As laughter mingles with every tear.

Here on this shore where smiles abound,
Even the sandcastles wear a crown.
With a wink from the moon, the day's end starts,
A horizon filled with whimsical hearts.

The Tapestry of Tranquil Waters

Waves like giggles, twinkling bright,
Splashing joy under the moonlight.
Sea turtles grooving, oh what a sight,
As starfish twirl, lost in delight.

A fisherman yawns, his catch is shy,
Baited hooks wearing a fun tie.
Marlin spins tales of grand escape,
While seaweed crafts hats in funny shape.

Splashing in calm, the kids rule the bay,
With laughter and bubbles, they dance and play.
A beach ball zips, veering off course,
As laughter erupts like a waving horse.

With each gentle tide, the island smiles,
In a comic show, it goes for miles.
In tranquil waters, our worries subside,
Wrapped in humor, forever our guide.

Notes from a Shell's Melodic Heart

A shell sings tunes of endless glee,
Its heartbeat dances, wild and free.
Seagulls laugh, with fishy wings,
While crabs on sand do silly things.

Turtles waddle in a funny race,
Chasing each other, a comical chase.
The sun sets low, with jellybean hues,
While snails wear hats, just to amuse.

Conch and clam share jokes galore,
Making waves with laughter's roar.
The ocean's a stage, what a sight,
With sea stars twinkling, pure delight.

So when you listen, don't be shy,
Grab a shell, and give it a try.
For laughter's a gift that you'll find,
Right in the ocean, fun intertwined.

Resilient Blooms by the Sea

Flowers sway in a windblown dance,
Catching sunbeams, taking a chance.
They poke their heads through sand and stone,
Wearing petals like party hats, grown.

Laughter drips from the salty air,
As sea oats giggle without a care.
A crab in a tux, what a sight to see,
In a land where the waves hold the key.

Palm trees twist in a playful spin,
While flocks of birds chime in the din.
The fragrance of fun, a cheerful tease,
Each blossom wearing a smile with ease.

So come join the blooms, revel and play,
For joy in the garden is here to stay.
With every splash and playful cheer,
Nature's the jokester, loud and clear.

Mysteries Beneath the Crescent Moon

The moon cackles, casting silver light,
Fish plot mischief, oh what a night!
Octopuses dress up for the ball,
While grinning dolphins perform for all.

Waves whisper secrets with giggles in tow,
As crabs tell tales of an old sea show.
Anemones wave, feeling quite spry,
Beckoning starfish, "Come give it a try!"

Beneath the waves, silliness reigns,
With coral blooms playing silly games.
The deep is alive with laughter and more,
Under the crescent, it's hard to ignore.

So if you dive in, take heed of the tune,
For the ocean's heart hums beneath the moon.
A world full of giggles, ease on your mind,
In the depths of night, humor you'll find.

Ember Hues of Dusk's Departure

As dusk arrives with ember flair,
The sky dons colors beyond compare.
Fishes leap, doing flips and splashes,
While sandcastles tumble in whimsical crashes.

Laughter echoes, the stars wink bright,
As shells play peek-a-boo, just out of sight.
The tide rolls in, bringing quirky shells,
With stories to tell, in joyful yells.

A pelican struts, wearing a grin,
As sea urchins chuckle, "Let's begin!"
The ocean's a stage with a wink and a nod,
Transforming each moment, oh! How it's awed!

So capture the fun before night consumes,
As nature spins tales in vibrant blooms.
The dusk bids farewell, but laughter stays,
In the heart of the sea, where joy always plays.

Dance of the Ocean's Caress

The waves wear smiles, oh what a sight,
Splashing near rocks, oh what a delight!
Seagulls are laughing, each flap a jest,
While sailors clumsily fail their best.

Crabs tap their feet on the sandy floor,
Bumping with shells, they dance and explore.
Even the fish join in with a laugh,
Chasing their tails on the ocean's behalf.

Sunbathers giggle, sunscreen in hand,
Avoiding the splash of the close by band.
A flip-flop flies, oh what a mishap,
Landing on toes for the perfect slap.

So if you find joy in a frolicsome wave,
Join in the fun, you'll see you're a slave.
To laugh with the tides is the best of the rest,
As the ocean's caress puts smiles to the test.

Secrets Carried by Seafoam

Whispers of shells tangled in seaweed,
Hold tales of crabs with their secret creed.
At high tide, they giggle, their laughter spills,
As they sneak past the shores with their little thrills.

The seafoam frolics, a mischievous sprite,
Tickling the toes of folks with delight.
An octopus juggles in a grand show,
While fish roll their eyes like, 'Oh, look at Joe!'

Sandcastles tumble, oh what a twist!
Waves gleefully claim them, did they exist?
Buried treasure? Just a sock, my friend,
Left behind from a beach day that won't end.

Secrets ride currents, so playful and sly,
Where mermaids might giggle, and dolphins will fly.
If laughter's the treasure that you wish to find,
Just listen to the sea, it's truly unkind!

Shadows Beneath the Coconut Canopy

Coconuts chuckle, oh what a view,
As they sway, they drop hints to the crew.
Squirrels play tag, scurrying quick,
Dodging the plummets, oh what a trick!

In multicolored hammocks, folks lay about,
Snoring and dreaming, with not much doubt.
The breeze starts to rustle, a tickle of fun,
As geckos perform in the midday sun.

A picnic unfolds, juice spills on the ground,
Laughter erupts, it's a wonderful sound.
Beach balls get struck, oh what a flight!
Into the bushes, they vanish from sight.

Just mind the coconuts hanging up high,
For when they tumble, oh me, oh my!
Yet here in the shade, without a care or scorn,
Life's just a circus, a game to adorn.

Above the Coral Sands

Kites dance like jellyfish, up in the blue,
While kids chase each other, as all children do.
With sand in their toes, they giggle away,
Constructing their dreams in a marvelous play.

A dog on a quest, chasing waves in delight,
Digs a big hole; it's a sandy fight!
His owner just laughs, what a sight to behold,
In the laughter of summer, joys manifold.

Sunsets arrive, painting skies all aglow,
As laughter rings out, it's a circus, you know!
The tide shows its wonders, with splashes and cheers,
A symphony played out, composed of all peers.

So come join the fun, leave your worries ashore,
For life here is filled with giggles galore.
With friends all around and the sun setting low,
Every moment's a treasure, just let your heart flow.

A Symphony of Waves and Whispers

The seagulls squawk, they steal my lunch,
While fish below, they try to munch.
A crab does the cha-cha, I can't keep my grin,
He wiggles and jives, he's got a win.

With coconuts bouncing, I try to surf,
But land on my belly, oh what a smurf!
Palm trees giggle, they sway with delight,
As I flounder around, what a glorious sight!

The sun's golden rays, oh what a tease,
They tickle my skin, bring goosebumps with ease.
A lizard joins in, he shows off his dance,
While I trip and tumble, what a clumsy chance!

In the sand, footprints draw a silly maze,
Where laughter erupts in silly displays.
The waves do their thing, a splashing parade,
As I sip my drink, lost in the cascade.

Radiant Horizons Beyond the Reef

Bright colored fish in a vibrant show,
Chasing sea turtles, oh how they flow.
With snorkel and flippers, I take a dive,
But a bubble escapes, do I still survive?

The dolphins are laughing, they jump in the air,
While I flounder about in my inflatable chair.
A whale gives a wink, it's a sight I can't miss,
As I splash in the waves, oh sweet ocean bliss.

The sunsets paint skies, a riot of hues,
As I argue with seagulls over my shoes.
They swoop and they soar, so cheeky and spry,
While I chase them around, oh me, oh my!

With drinks in our hands, we dance on the shore,
As crabs try to join in, but fall with an oar.
Tonight, we celebrate waves and their charms,
Laughing on sands, with our hearts left unarmed.

Where the Sky Meets the Sea

From the dock, I wave, to the boat in the bay,
While it drifts away, oh please don't stray!
The fishermen chuckle as I make a run,
For a fish that got away—was it really that fun?

The clouds look like llamas, all fluffy and white,
While jellyfish dance, a clear jelly delight.
With sunscreen applied, I become a fine sight,
Reflecting the sun, oh what a bright plight!

Seagulls swoop down, eyeing my snack,
With one false move, they might attack!
I guard my sandwich with a stern, funny frown,
As they plot their strike, I'll take them down!

The waves crash and tumble, they giggle and play,
While I imagine they hold a party today.
With laughter and joy, we run down the shore,
For in this wild fun, who could ask for more?

Vibrations of a Tranquil Heart

The ukulele strums, a joyful refrain,
While we dance on the beach, dodging the rain.
A coconut falls, with a thud at my feet,
But my laughter erupts, oh what a sweet treat!

With sunscreen globbed on, looking quite grand,
I skip down the shore, with a drink in my hand.
The tide pulls away, but not without glee,
As I tumble and roll like a leaf from a tree.

The hibiscus blossoms sway just so,
While I shake my maracas with a wild show.
A parrot squawks jokes, what a feisty bird,
Mimicking laughter, that's truly absurd!

With friends all around, the sun starts to set,
We'll dance 'til the stars, no sign of regret.
For joy fills the air, with each giggle and cheer,
In this tranquil heart, we chase off our fear.

Moonlit Tides and Tropical Melodies

Beneath the glow of a bright moon's gaze,
The crabs do the cha-cha, caught in a daze.
Coconuts giggle, swaying on their vines,
While fish throw a disco, in shimmering lines.

The waves hum a tune, silly and sweet,
As turtles tap dance on their little webbed feet.
Palm fronds sway, waving, they join in the fun,
Even the stars twinkle, our party's begun!

With laughter and joy, we gather around,
Listening to tales of the sea and the sound.
An octopus DJ spins records with flair,
While seagulls squawk rhymes that float through the air.

As night deepens, shadows begin to tease,
Pineapple piñatas hang from the trees.
We swing with our laughter, no care for the tide,
In this silly dance, with our friends by our side.

Heartbeats of the Island Heart

With a bounce in the step and a beat in the chest,
We're running in circles, who knows who is best?
Bananas are slipping, oh what a surprise,
The laughter erupts, as the coconut flies!

Mangoes are juggling, oh look at them soar,
While lizards throw parties outside every door.
The rhythm is contagious, come join in the cheer,
Even the palm trees mumble, 'We want a beer!'

We've tied up our shoes, it's a wild clam bake,
With a dash of salt water for flavor, no fake.
The heartbeats echo, like drums in the night,
As we roast sweet potatoes and giggle in fright.

So come dance with us, let your worries take flight,
With the beat of the island, it feels so right.
In this raucous fun, let the good times abound,
For the heart of the island beats joyfully loud!

Starlit Paths Through Swaying Grasses

Under the starlight, a twinkling parade,
With grass tickling toes, what a grand escapade.
The crickets are crooning a symphony strange,
While the owls hoot out notes that seem to rearrange.

Fireflies twinkle like candy on strings,
Catching our laughter, oh how it sings!
A duet of shadows on this grassy floor,
Watch out for the frogs, they're ready for war!

Each step brings a jig, a hop and a skip,
As the moon spills like honey from its sweet lip.
We tumble and roll, with no fear of the night,
Our fears are all silly, lost in delight.

So join in the fun, don't mind the grass stains,
For every misstep, there's joy that remains.
With starlit paths beckoning, we stroll side by side,
In the heart of the night, let your worries slide!

Whirlwinds of Island Folklore

Gather 'round, hear the legends retold,
Of mermaids who sing and pirates who scold.
Octopuses dance in a flurry of rhymes,
As the wind plays its tricks with the coconut limes.

The pineapple prince rode on waves made of cream,
While the monkeys concocted a wild, scrumptious dream.
With tales of mischief, like fish in a net,
They'll wave with a wink, 'Oh, you haven't seen yet!'

A flamingo in socks, tap dancing with flair,
While turtles play bingo without any care.
The island is chuckling, it's a jubilant mess,
We join in the laughter; oh, what a success!

So raise up your cups, let the stories pour free,
With whimsy and wonder, come share it with me.
In the whirlwinds of folklore, where laughter won't tire,
Let the tales become treasures, we'll dance by the fire!

www.ingramcontent.com/pod-product-compliance
Lightning Source LLC
Chambersburg PA
CBHW050317100526
44585CB00016BA/1496